the
back
door

Copyright © 2000 by Carl DeLine
All rights reserved

Canadian Cataloguing in Publication Data

DeLine, Carl David, 1950-
  The Back Door

ISBN 1-55056-791-8

1. Street youth--Services for--Calgary. I. Back Door
(Calgary, Alta.) II. Title
HV4510.C3D44 2001   362.74   C00-911488-2

Published by *the back door*
        Calgary, Alberta, Canada

First printing 2001
Second printing 2001
Printed and bound in Canada by   Friesens Corporation
                           Altona, Manitoba

Contents

Foreword

Are young people on the street any different from other young people? Do they share the same hopes and aspirations as young people off the streets?

Many people who design programs and create programs do so as if there is very little difference. The young people who have been a part of *the back door* dispel this myth in many ways. The differences are immense. Yet, these same young people became an encouragement to the hopes of many in our society. This world can be a better place. Time and again a young person who is on the street makes the decision to start their journey toward a new direction. They take hold of every opportunity to rewrite their lives and make it work to leave the violence and addictions of the street world behind them. Every step away from the street is a new experiment. There are no promises as to where the journey will lead. There are no magic wands that instantly make everything better. There is a lot of hard work. For every successful step there are many failures. But in each case the ultimate conclusion leads to a safer and stronger sense of purpose and life.

the back door started by helping to point young people towards jobs. Over the years *the back door* has helped young people who are coming off the street to integrate into a new life, to move beyond jobs to a fuller understanding of making life off the street work.

Dedication

To the participants, it is their willingness to experiment
that continually opens new doors.

THE BACK DOOR, A YOUTH EMPLOYMENT SOCIETY

Why this book, at this time?
Because:
1. People from other cities are asking what it would take to have a *back door* in their city or community.
2. Evaluators have said that, *the back door* has not only enabled many young people to change their lives, but the program itself may well serve as a model for other kinds of social transitions.*
3. Evaluators have also said that, "*the back door* program has several unusual features which distinguish it from other programs with similar aims. For example, *the back door* program places an unusual level of responsibility on the individual participant. This high level of individual responsibility extends to the selection of goals, pacing of the program, and the means selected by participants to resolve for themselves the step-by-step transition away from the streets." It is the frustration of many street people that so many programs which have been developed to help them have only resulted in a revolving door which often leads back to the street. This frustration will continue until both the street and the non-street recognize the need to bridge the cultural gaps. *the back door* bridges those gaps.
4. In the midst of all that is said and written about street people, many non-street people still believe the myth that young people choose the street for some glamorous or adventurous reason. In reality, the vast majority of young people who have come to *the back door* refute this idea as they publicly back up their intentions with their efforts to get off and stay off the street.

*additional thoughts on pg. 68 Pacific Rim Research Team

What We Do Today

For/with young street people (the participant)

We call ourselves a youth employment project. In reality this isn't necessarily true. The name came about because funding bodies need a way to identify us. Since employment is the end goal, it is easy to say we focus on employment. It was discovered over time that *the back door* is an integration project. Young people from the ages of 17 to 24 who are part of the street culture come to us. Our choice to designate the ages of 17 to 24 arose out of the lack of programs for that age group in the city of Calgary at the time we started. It is the goal of each youth to get off the street. If they are to get off the street, and stay off the street, they need to join the non-street culture/society as a potentially employable person. If they are not employable then they need to become a part of a support system which deals with both their survival and developmental needs.

At present, there are 100 young people who are contracting with *the back door*. Contracting means that each person who has identified his/her desire to get off the street will begin to create what becomes the first step away from the street. Each month they will create eight identifiable steps to move away from the street. In a 12 month period up to 100 steps will be identified and worked on.

Each young person enters into the contract process in the following way:

1. The young person on the street identifies a desire to say "I want to get off the street."
2. This thought process continues with the potential participant seeking out *the back door.*
3. Once the potential participant states this desire to get off the street and they come to *the back door,* a contract process is started.
4. The participant then identifies a step which will point him or her away from the street.
5. The participant enters this step into the computer and/or on a contract sheet, creating what becomes a contract.
6. The participant discusses this step with a volunteer or staff person identifying, in non-street words, what this contract is about.
7. The participant then receives a $15 bonus for having created this contract. The money is paid when the participant creates the contract not after it is carried out.
8. After leaving *the back door's* offices the participant comes back to *the back door,* discusses the success or failure of the said contract step, and begins to create yet another contract.

The non-street world believes in perks and bonuses. We call this $15 a bonus. Each person will qualify for up to eight bonuses in a month and no more than 100 bonuses in a 12 month period, with a maximum of 24 months of contracting.

Each step is identified as a part of the plan which will point the contractee (participant) away from the street. The steps can be in one of the following categories:

1. **housing**: steps taken toward obtaining an appropriate, safe, independent living situation with landlord negotiation as required, and appropriate life style issues addressed.
2. **jobs**: any steps which address issues related to preparation for and obtaining employment and dealing appropriately with problems arising within the job situation.

3. **education**: steps taken toward educational assessment, academic upgrading and planning for work.

4. **personal**: any steps taken to deal with personal life concerns and coping, e.g. relationships, attitudes, appearance.

5. **planning**: thinking, formulating possible action/alternatives in the area of life concerns.

6. **volunteer work**: giving of one's own time and effort to contribute back to a community which is supportive of the participant.

7. **finances**: any steps to acquire knowledge or principles of action relating to money management or awareness of spending philosophy.

8. **legal**: steps taken to deal with past or current legal concerns to ensure their appropriate expedition, therefore enabling freedom to pursue the changes in life necessary to move off the street.

9. **leadership**: formal involvement in coaching, supporting by active example, or participation with others in positive movement in areas of life concerns.

10. **drug/alcohol**: any step taken to acknowledge the reality of personal substance abuse and to address issues of rehabilitation (for example, detox or participation in twelve step type programs).

11. **problem solving**: steps representing any thought or action given to defining the problem, seeking alternative solutions, acting upon this, and processing the outcome.

12. **identification**: obtaining acceptable identification as necessary to integrate into the community.

13. **other**: any steps not specifically designated in the above categories but which deal with issues and concerns critical to the participant in his/her movement off the street.

Contracting remains the basis of communication at *the back door*. A young person comes to us because he/she wants to get off the street. Once this is identified a step is then developed. This step remains an activity which continues to point the participant in the direction away from the street. At first this step will usually deal with a crisis or an immediate identified need. In time the participant will begin to contract with longer term goals in mind.

The following table is an illustration of what the contract page looks like. A crucial understanding is the amount of flexibility on the part of either the staff person or volunteer. If the staff or volunteer gets too involved in the contract, the contract then no longer belongs to the participant. If the participant does not have ownership of his/her contract, accountability becomes more and more of a problem. Over the years the percentages of contracts relate to the 13 categories as follows:

Housing	11%	Planning	6%	Drugs/Alcohol	5%
Employment	22%	Volunteering	2%	Problem Solving	3%
Education	8%	Finances	9%	Identification	3%
Personal	19%	Leadership	1%	Legal	5%
Other	6%				

COPY OF CONTRACT PAGE:

the back door
MAKING CHANGE
Name:

                                          Date:
                                          File #

...Housing	...Planning	...Drugs/Alcohol
...Employment	...Volunteering	...Problem Solving
...Education	...Finances	...Identification
...Personal	...Leadership	...Legal
		...Other

CONTRACT STEP: Step#:

WHAT I WANT TO WORK ON TODAY i.e. WHERE I AM TODAY IN MY LIFE

WHAT RESULT(S) I WOULD LIKE TO SEE i.e. WHERE I WOULD LIKE TO BE

WHAT I NEED TO MAKE IT WORK:

MY STEPS:
        1
        2
        3
        4

Contractor: Paid by:

The following principles & questions reflect how *the back door* hopes to work. Please take time to think about how they worked worked for you in THIS contract step.

1. Principle: INTEGRITY/DIGNITY
...How did contracting this step contribute positively to your self esteem?
2. Principle: life is such that things do not always work
...In attempting the above step how did you find this to be so?
3. Principle: ACCEPTANCE WITHOUT JUDGMENT OR PREJUDICE
...How did contracting this step allow you to experience positive input from another person?
4. Principle: FORGIVENESS: EVERY DAY IS A NEW DAY
...How did contracting this step give you the freedom to learn from the past and try again?
5. Principle:PEOPLE WHO LISTEN TO EACH OTHER LEARN FROM EACH OTHER
..How did planning/working on this step help you to understand another person's point of view?
6. Principle: ALL ACTIONS/CHOICES AFFECT OTHER PEOPLE
...Did your working on this step have any effect on other people in your life?

For/with non-street volunteers

If a young person is to move into the non-street world they must have entry points. These entry points must be nurtured by non-street people who live the non-street every day. It is imperative that the non-street person then integrate new understandings of the street world as they are informed by the participants. As they learn about the street they will understand what is necessary for a young person to make such a transition.

The aforementioned contract is with *the back door,* not with a counselor. *the back door* does not have staff who have a caseload. Volunteers do not come in and take on a caseload, nor are they a "buddy." Each volunteer becomes a conduit of non-street experience, wisdom and knowledge. That is why it is so important for participants to meet and contract with as many non-street people as possible. In fact, to increase the opportunities for communication, the person the participant contracts with and the person who pays him are in most cases not the same. This allows contact with at least two non-street people on each occasion of contracting.

Each non-street person is in *the back door* environment for one of four reasons. These reasons are:

> 1. The contractor (staff/volunteer) has said they want to help if they can. They are not at *the back door* to give advice. They are there to listen to the participant and interpret what they are hearing from the participant into non-street words. It is imperative that the participant learns words/language which will help them to communicate in the non-street world. As each participant learns the words of the non-street culture they begin to understand what it is they need to know in order to take ownership of their objective to get off the street.
> 2. The contractor is there to ask participants questions so they can learn and understand the street culture. In so doing, the telling of a story by a participant enables the participant to identify their own path off the street. Each

non-street person or contractor has their entire life experience to offer as a resource for survival and growth. "In my world this means..."

3. The contractors provide help on the computer. Each participant will develop his/her own contract on the computer. By learning basic computer skills the participants learn skills which help them to access other educational venues. The computer is also functionally objective, allowing the discussion between the contractor and participant to be focused on something other than the stress of identifying goals and processes. At times, a participant is contracted with by *the back door* to teach new volunteers or contractors about contracting. By doing this, the contracting process becomes a natural part of the thought process of the participant.

4. Contractors also work on research. Each contractor prepares thoughts on street issues and then attempts to put them into words which will help other non-street people understand the process of getting off the street. Contractors will also identify their own path of coming to understand the street. As this is done, a greater appreciation of the strengths and weaknesses of both cultures is identified.

History: How *the back door* came about

the back door as a project must be placed into the context of many events. These events go back as far as 1984/1985. At that time the Food Bank received considerable visibility. A great deal of pressure was put on the Social Welfare departments to respond to the growing numbers of people who were coming to the Food Bank. Both Calgarys' City and Edmontons' City Social Services research departments observed that young people comprised approximately 30% of those who were coming to their respective food banks. City Social Services prepared a document indicating that many people coming to the Food Bank showed no income at all. In addition, upon further investigation, the population of potentially employable young individuals consistently indicated no income. Their records at the Food Bank indicated "no fixed address" and the statement "awaiting Unemployment Insurance".

Because of this information both the Deputy Minister and the Minister of Social Services at that time began to act. The Regional Director for the Calgary area was assigned a brief stint at the Food Bank to verify the validity of the situation. His overall conclusions, which were communicated to us at the Food Bank and then back to the Minister, verified that in fact, the Food

Bank was helping those who stood outside the activity of the Social Welfare Department. The Deputy Minister asked to have a Community Council formed which was done. Many community agencies, including City Social Services and Alberta Social Services, were represented. As the dialogue continued, a group of persons were identified who moved back and forth between the Food Bank and other agencies seeking help. Young, single, potentially employable persons kept falling through the cracks in the system.

The province and city stopped funding the youth employment projects run by community groups. City Social Services then designed the Youth Employment Centre in order to address the issue of youth employment - including street youth. Provincial funds which would have gone to community groups were then earmarked for the city project.

Unfortunately, the transient population, due to lack of stable housing and various addictions, did not qualify for the type of services being offered by this new project. Avenue 15, which was created by the Boys and Girls Club prior to this, only served people under 17 years of age. The Single Men's Hostel and the Drop In Centre were the primary places for single unemployed people over 17. Due to funding cuts and staff shortages these places could only be used for a bed or a mattress. If someone needed a place to make phone calls in response to jobs listed in the newspaper or a place to do longer term planning, this was not available. People were asked to leave these places in the morning and not come back until suppertime. The street became a refuge for many.

The daily press covered the aforementioned discussions and spoke out concerning the urgency of needs whenever possible. There was an increasing awareness by many in the community of what was happening.

Due to the work at the Food Bank, much discussion was generated in the community around the issues of employment and unemployment. In fact, the growing concern was illustrated in then Deputy Minister Michael Ozerkovich's presentation *The Impact of Structural Change* at the Passages 2000 conference. Many agencies participated in this conference. The provincial government began on a ministerial level to discuss the way in which Alberta Social Services and the Alberta Career Development & Employment could work more closely. Many conversations took place among community people, the ministers, the Mayor's office, caucus members, and their respective support staffs before *the back door* even got started.

This becomes an important part of the history because *the back door* arose out of both community and government dialogue. It was accepted by both sectors that if something were to be developed, the typical methods would not work. In addition to this, traditional funding sources such as government, United Way, and local foundations had identified that this population was not included in their mandates. Traditional approaches to both method and funding simply were not working.

The question which ultimately arose out of these conversations was: who would deal with, or take ownership of the problems concerning youth on the street?

Due to the efforts of the Edmonton Social Planning Council and Edmonton Social Services, these reports became public. The question was then asked "what is the cost of getting a young person off the street?" An unpublished report written by myself and a team of people following conversations with a private foundation was then prepared and presented for consideration. It was out of this research that *the back door* was created. Originally *the back door* was started under the umbrella of the Calgary Interfaith Community Action Association and was called 'Calgary Interfaith-A Youth Employment Society'.

The analysis from this unpublished report included interviews with front line workers from over 50 different cities and over five different countries. In all cases, very key points developed around location, integration and assimilation. Each interview asked the question: "if money were no object, if you could wave a magic wand, what would you (the street worker) do?" Overwhelming responses came back suggesting a totally different approach. Instead of maintaining a process where individuals are constantly a part of the street world, it was suggested that the starting point should be away from the street.

As the research developed it became apparent that dignity, self esteem and respect were constant variables in most conversations. So also was the inability to access the necessary cash to survive. How were young people to effect the transition from the street to the non-street with dignity, self esteem and respect? With encouragement from an anonymous donor the "pay for performance" bonus concept was introduced. It was recognized that pay for performance was an essential component of our economy. Since this was the case, it was determined that "pay for performance" might work for street youth as well in the enhancement of dignity, self esteem and respect. Why not try this as an alternative to handouts. The bonus concept was developed as clean money. No strings were attached as payments were "earned" by the participant. The contract was created as a way to encourage accountability, not to a system, but to oneself.

the back door declared a mandate. It would choose to work with both young people who want to get off the street and potential staff and volunteers who want to help young people in their transition. This was to be done on an experimental basis. For the first year the entire funding would be provided by a private anonymous donor. At the end of the first year evaluative steps would be taken at which time the foundation's criteria for continued funding was that *the back door* was to show a balance of support which could include potential government funding. An agreement ensued with both Career Development and Employment and Social Services. Once again it is important to realize that this provincial funding was provided even though both Career Development and Employment and Social Services acknowledged "We've never done it that way before."

the back door was developed as an experimental pilot project. The first location for *the back door* was 90 blocks outside of the downtown core on the light rapid transit (LRT) system. Public transportation away from the street *milieu* was viewed as imperative. Staff were then hired based on a multi-disciplinary approach. A social worker, a school teacher, and a business person were selected. With this team it was believed that as many aspects of the contracting process could be dealt with as possible.

On Jan. 1, 1988 *the back door* opened. Youth who were living on the street were recruited by word of mouth. Each young person was asked if he/she would be interested in participating in an experiment. If it worked, he/she got off the street. If it didn't work then he/she would be no worse off than before. During 1988, 30 participants began with *the back door*.

Participants-who they are and where they come from

During the first year, the policy was to accept only individuals who had been on the street for at least four years. As the program developed it was recognized that if a person had been on the street for a shorter period of time, it was actually easier to get settled off the street. When we first started *the back door*, over 90% of the participants had been placed into child welfare by the age of five. By the age of 14 some had been moved around to as many as 200 foster care homes. The average person was on the street by the age of 14. By the time they got to us they typically had five years of life skills training on the street. They were clearly integrated into a sub-culture that has a whole different set of values and perspectives than the non-street.

To persons living in the street sub-culture, the enemy is clearly defined; it is the non-street. For instance, the street perceives the non-street as evil and not to be trusted. *If an opportunity to take advantage of the non-street sector was available, the street person would consider it a crime not to take advantage of a non-street person.*

This understanding is deeply rooted in the survival mentality of the street.

Discovering the cost

One of the original intentions of this project was to discover the cost of integrating an individual from the street culture into mainstream society. Integration is a settlement process for street youth. Street youth are migrant and lack the basic skills and understanding required to assimilate into the non-street society. An understanding of why certain behaviors are, or are not, acceptable just is not there. We have often argued for a new way of thinking: pre-entry to pre-entry.

This acknowledges that most pre-entry programs take for granted a certain level of enculturation. Pre-entry says you must clean up before you can participate. Due to the lack of funding and programming directed toward this population, each individual person has often been told simply to "go out and find a job." The fact that a person may not be ready to take a job and keep it was often not taken into consideration. Getting the job rather then keeping the job became more important than discovering how employable a person was and helping them develop the capabilities to keep a job.

To understand the cost of moving a person off the street, it must be understood that a wide range of variables exist. When we first started, the majority of our participants needed immediate medical attention. Such conditions as open sores, bruises, wounds, bad teeth, bleeding gums, rashes, poor eye sight and poor nutrition were common. In addition, not having a health care card, or a legal address only made matters worse. Getting care and becoming settled was complicated because of the system's inability to respond.

Without a legal address a person could not get the care necessary to be presentable to access an education or a job. Because our participants had been around and around in this process, they had absolutely no reason to believe that things would now be different. Why should they trust *the back door*? *the back door* had to nurture a trust process. This was done by going with a participant to medical treatment, to the social welfare office, to a potential employer, to act as an advocate and to offer *the back door's* address as a usable address. In time the reputation of *the back door* was sufficient. If a person was identified as being with *the back door*, it gave entrance to certain programs. In one situation it was working so well that a participant stole a box of staff business cards and was selling them on the street for $20 each. We found this out when an employer called and told us he had hired one of our guys. We did not recognize the name of the person presenting the card to this employer. The employer then asked him where he got the business card. He said he had bought it for $20 on the street. When the employer said he was going to fire this guy for his dishonesty we urged the employer to give this fellow a chance. After all, we pointed out, when was the last time someone paid money to get an interview with you? Just give him a chance. We found out who stole the cards and dealt with it on our own.

As *the back door* began to partner with other community groups in setting up a health care clinic, housing resources, and a network of community agencies, another twist developed. The community at large began to say to *the back door*, figure out what you want to do, help street kids, do medical work, do housing, do jobs, do education - you can't do it all. Narrow your focus. When you do, then we will decide to which of these concerns we will give money. While we were friendly with workers and administrators in the system, we were constantly being told that funding mandates were not allowed to cross disciplines. This was also true when other funding sources were approached. In the first three years we made over 20,000 appeals for funding. The consistent reason for not getting funding was that our mandate was too broad.

In answering the question of costs, the cost of moving a young person off the street became equal to the bonus money plus the cost of *the back door* expenses pro-rated per participant. In addition, whatever non-*back door* moneys were needed to heal, train, dress up or prepare the participant for whatever part of the non-street world they were going into, would be added to determine the total real cost.

Belief Systems

Belief systems exist, and behavior ensues.

In discussing the belief system of *the back door*, it may seem logical to accept the idea that differing belief systems exist, hence a *back door* belief system also exists. However, it is imperative to not overlook or take for granted that behaviors are dictated by one's belief system. Because belief systems exist, they can be identified behaviorally in cultures, sub-cultures, groupings and individuals.

Both the street and the non-street have unique and discernible belief systems. At *the back door* <u>the street and the non-street begin on equal footings.</u> Both have their right to exist there because both areas of life exist. Off the street, it is not uncommon for one to deny the right of the other to exist. Young people end up on the street because of brokenness in their own lives. They stay on the street because society is broken. How these two subcultures live together, how they understand one another, how people move back and forth in these subcultures are all concerns which *the back door* deals with daily.

Philosophical Roots: 5 Major Points

The belief system of *the back door* is predicated upon a number of philosophical viewpoints. *the back door* is a community project and it arose out of a philosophical dialogue concerning perceived inadequacies in the systems that deal with street youth. At the same time, like other programs, whether education, social welfare, hospital or medicine, it found its origin in a faith community.

At *the back door* one concern is the development of a process whereby the theological influences which shaped the origins of *the back door* can always be in dialogue with, and respected by, the community. The funding community has a tendency to say that the philosophy or belief system of the project is secondary to funding. At *the back door* we have said the founding principles are pre-eminent. Any funding then respects the principles which created the program and the integrity of the program.

5 major points

1. All people are created with integrity.
Integrity is not something that a person earns by virtue of his/her behavior or actions. Integrity is something that a person has simply by virtue of his/her having been created. At *the back door* integrity is the word that allows us to respect a person as they are. At *the back door* a person has a right to exist the way they are without being told how they have to conform. Behavior is not the reason for acceptance. The fact is, the person exists with whatever life experiences they bring with them. The dilemma comes when behavior is used as the criteria to judge who a person is. At *the back door*, we say the person is separate from his/her behavior. We do not ignore the person's behavior, but we say the starting point is that he or she is to be accepted as a person of integrity: no matter who it is that walks in the door.

2. All people are broken to some degree and in some way.
It is an understanding at *the back door* that all persons need to recognize that facets of their own lives are broken. Because of this, all persons, no matter who they are, fall short of a sense of

16

wholeness as people. Once a person gives him/herself the right to overlook their own brokenness a destructive judgmental spirit dominates. It is then very common for negative judgments to be made and to influence the way decisions are made about others. When this happens the person being judged is not defined by who they are as a person but rather how they measure up to the expectations of the judge. To be absolutely right, the judge must be absolutely perfect in his/her judgments. At *the back door* we have chosen to believe that this perfect judge does not exist. In fact, we acknowledge that the influence of one's environment conditions one's role or place in society. Society defines its own laws, its own dictates, its own policies and its own procedures. These laws define who/what is good or bad. Any one who does not think in the same way or who does not live up to the predetermined procedures, policies or practices, is automatically defined as wrong or bad.

What we have recognized at *the back door* is that our society is made up of a massive number of sub-cultures. These sub-cultures create their own laws and ways to carry out these laws. Once this is recognized, it is easy to understand that any one person has the potential of fitting into a particular society in a very positive way. When placed into another society, he or she may be deemed or perceived negatively.

It is very clear for *the back door* that people who come to *the back door* do not measure up to common interpretations of acceptable standards in society. The brokenness of each person's life is a given at *the back door*. All people fall short of the laws or ethics and values held by our society. All people are broken.

3. Forgivingness is the ability to pick oneself up and to start over time and time again.

Forgiveness isn't one person saying to another, "You did something bad. I forgive you." At *the back door* forgiveness arises out of an understanding that a person cannot live up to certain laws or expectations. At times these laws become so internalized and powerful that a person stumbles over the smallest expectations. A person finds him/herself standing alone because certain dictates cannot be lived up to. Certain things just can't be done. One of the most difficult aspects of forgiveness is not one person forgiving another, it is the ability of one person to forgive themselves and to ultimately accept themselves. It is recognizing that this acceptance is the starting point and life can and must be built on such a simple concept. Building one's future has nothing to do with loving oneself but rather acknowledging that a starting point to build upon has been provided for each of us. Integrity, hence ultimately human dignity, is based on having been created. As such, failure simply provides an opportunity to start over.

So it is that when a young person uses his/her body in prostitution, drug abuse or other criminally defined behaviors there comes a sense of defilement. This sense of defilement causes one to say I am wrong instead of saying my behavior is wrong. I cannot be changed. I cannot be made right. I cannot be made whole. This sense of defilement seems to build from one experience to another. As the young person enters one subculture after another they see how far short they fall compared to the perceived laws and practices in each of these subcultures.

It isn't long before there is a feeling of worthlessness. In the first year of *the back door* we conducted a series of tests on participants. Each of the participants was contracted to do a Taylor-Johnson Temperament Analysis. All except one of the participants, on a self-worth scale of 1 to 10, scored 1 (1 being lowest). One participant scored a four. I brought that young man into my office and asked him questions about how deeply he was involved in the street. Out of our discussion it was discovered that he really was on the fringe of the street. He was the person who stood behind the tree and watched the fight. Once the fight was finished, he would jump in and say that he had been part of the battle. If there was a drug deal going down, he was the person who stood in the background and waited for the deal to happen. He then showed up as if he had been part of the whole thing. He had all the words but little of the action. He was not committed to the violence or to the criminal behavior of the street. He was committed simply to being part of a group of people within the street itself. In many ways he was not a part of the degradation of the street. The others wore their 'defilement'. The others knew what it was to have violence done to them and to do it to others as well.

Forgiveness is extremely difficult to experience on the street because once a person begins to feel a sense of worthlessness, then they continue to degrade themselves time and again.

At *the back door* we choose simply to say that it is okay to start over. It is okay to say to one's self that it is time to begin to build life in a new way. It is time to begin to understand that forgiveness is not based on a moral response or belief system. While there are many other words used to discuss forgiveness, forgiveness will never be understood until a person is willing to take the next step in a new direction. In the context of *the back door* <u>forgivingness</u> is the ability to pick oneself up and to start over time and time again.

4. An incarnational dialogue is needed.
This and the following point do not relate to the participants as much as they relate to non-street people. The role of the non-street person is to walk alongside of the street person. It is the beginning of an incarnational dialogue. This commands the non-street person to get into the head, the thinking, the life experience of the participant without patronizing or pitying the participant. As the non-street person hears the participant's story they are to give those words back to the participant in such a way that the participant hears his/her own words and understands that they have been heard. This becomes a basis for understanding what truth is all about. The truth is that you said you wanted to get off the street. When a person comes to *the back door* and participates in *the back door*, the very first contract step is to say, "I want to get off the street."

The street nurtures lies and untruths. The street does not live with a tomorrow. The street lives for the here and now. Take what you can, when you can. The street person lives with an understanding of one day, a 24 hour period of time. In fact this is often more appropriately 12 hours at a time. Everything is based on a pragmatic 'now'. The street person has absolutely no reason to believe in truth as presented by the non-street or street world. It is imperative that a non-street person create a basis of understanding from which to understand the participant's story. To understand where the participant is coming from will allow the non-street person the ability to ask "where are you going? and "how do you plan to get there?" This turns the story back into the hands of the participant and allows ownership and truth ultimately to be nurtured.

Truth begins to be understood when one tiny particle of it can be built on and a *truth process* can be built on that one particle. When the contract is developed, the participants are held accountable for their own words. Once the participants say that they want to get off the street, and once they take ownership for their own words, (which usually takes 3 or 4 months in the contracting process) it is then that the participants begin to develop an image of their own sense of integrity. Dignity then arises out of the ability to see one's own success. It grows from the tiniest understanding to become a platform which can be built upon.

The non-street person must earn his or her right to be understood, to be a listener, and to be a giver in the continuing process. The non-street person - just like the participant - must learn what their own words are about. These words cannot be "It should be like this, or like that." The words must be, "Help me understand". As the non-street person looks deep inside themselves, he/she does not confront or dialogue out of perceived realities or understandings. Instead the realities of their own life experiences, the forgiveness he or she has experienced, the failures he or she has experienced as well as the successes and the joys in his/her own life become the basis for direction.

   5. Help is based on an immediate response, not long term planning.
The response of the staff or volunteer is to nurture a thought process which deals with the crisis at hand. It is not appropriate

to give advice, problem solve or suggest how the participant should feel. Help must take the form of listening and asking questions which initiate the participants's own thought processes. For this to work, the staff or volunteer must relate intuitively, authentically, and in a manner consistent with their own belief systems. The nature of the street creates crisis. Time for planning is a luxury. The non-street person must understand that a longer term plan often has to be set aside to deal with what is urgent. In fact the long term plan may be so altered it can not be returned to and the participant will need to start with a new plan. This final point creates a challenge for a world based on professionalism. We live in a society where professionalism has often become one of its own worst enemies. In many ways, the very systems which have been created now block the ability of the professional to serve. At *the back door,* the non-street person has the task of learning how to serve with no strings attached. There is only room to say, "If I can help I will. If I can't, I will stay out of your way". The street person lives with too many urgencies to take up residence in the non-street world. The street person has too many other people putting demands on him or her, sabotaging their own process. Once the person has been contracting and gets more settled, only then will longer term plans be made. As a participant begins to measure one step at a time, initiative is nurtured. Starting over becomes natural.

"This is your life." These words go both ways. It is a given fact that just as the participant needs to have his or her integrity/dignity intact, so does the person doing the contracting on behalf of *the back door.* This contract cannot violate the belief system of the contractor. This becomes another crucial point. A primary difference between *the back door* and many other agencies is that the policies of other agencies have a tendency to define what is or is not an acceptable belief system for staff or volunteers. At *the back door* we nurture an environment that allows a person to come with a sense of self. He or she does not dialogue a contracting process out of a prescribed belief system developed by *the back door.* The freedom to be who he/she is as a person in real life takes precedence.

We are not at *the back door* to convert people to think and to believe some predetermined belief system. We are there to say, "Learn that in our world and in our society there are many different belief systems." If a participant is going to make it off the street he or she is going to have to learn how to live in a world with all of those different belief systems. The participant will need to nurture their instincts in order to move into a new world. The only criteria for contracting is that the contract points in a direction away from a livelihood on the street.

Philosophical Nuances
Street and non-street cultures exist

The philosophy of the non-street world arises out of the culture or the subcultures in which people live. Variables and dynamics dealing with such things as the acquisition of personal belongings and human relationships exist in each culture. Each culture or subculture chooses its own set of values which it will adhere to. Once a society's belief systems are accepted they become policies and norms which ultimately lead to some form of codifying behavior and law.

Societies and cultures may choose to live to the letter of its own law, or it may choose to be more flexible and live to the intent but not the letter of the law.

It is imperative to recognize how people choose to live and adapt to the communities where they live, work, and seek a quality of life. It is also important to understand how various pressures affect the decision making process. It isn't just what people believe, but how they live because of what they believe. This is true of people in business, schools, churches, community groups, or wherever. If you are a part of a family, a clan or a neighborhood you represent one of the millions of belief systems, cultures or subcultures that exist around the world.

At *the back door* we must go the next step. Once the street person says they want off the street we continue to express the need of continually joining the non-street. We have to be very clear to ask which part of the non-street world the participant wants to join.

Just as the non-street has its subcultures and governing philosophies of life so does the street. The street is based on an autocratic structure. There are very clear forms of authority. There are very clear neighborhoods or turfs. When someone is new and they move to a new street corner they must take the time to understand what is already in place. For instance, when somebody is already doing street business from a particular street corner any new street person has to seek permission to be in that space. The street has its own form of market economy. It is the purest form of market anywhere. On the street everything is for sale (including a person's body if need be).

The street is part of a dominance oriented or violence orientated culture. It tells people how they should act. It pressures people into a process that dictates what to believe and then supports the process with a lifestyle that literally destroys the people in it. A facade of freedom often lures people into a life of enslavement and oppression which allows one merely to survive on the street. Getting out of the street environment may mean moving one rapid step at a time in any direction possible. Flight from the street often means running into the non-street world and experiencing closed doors. With anxiety, compulsivity and the need to survive, the street person will move as doors are opened, in many cases stepping through the available door only to find out that it is not the right door to go through.

When someone asks to move away from the street, that person must also come to grips with why they are choosing to get off the street. Often it is not because of money, it is not because of circles of people, it is usually to get away from the violence of the street. *the back door* does not pretend the non-street is without violence. We do suggest however, that it has a value base which says there should be less violence.

23

There is a tremendous amount of paranoia in the street world. The line between real fears and imagined fears has become very blurred. Street people are always looking over their shoulder, always wondering who might be there to challenge them, always wondering if someone from the law is after them, always wondering if the person they have connected with may be in trouble with the law. One never knows when authorities of some type can come breaking into your world and can challenge your space. Once a person begins to view life from this type of perspective, the next steps develop easily: a sense of arrogance, a hardening, a searing not only of their conscience, but of their attitudes and the way they treat others. Once that searing happens, there is a movement toward rebellious attitudes which are needed just to survive. "I can stand outside your world." "I don't need you people." Rebellion should not always be seen as a violent response or an aggressive response. On the street, rebellion is often just a way of surviving.

We start by asking the young person to begin the process of understanding the culture they are about to move into. What does this culture believe about the length of your hair, the colour of your hair, the jewelry on your face and your body, the style of clothing, the colour of your clothing, how often that clothing is washed, whether it is clean, or carries an odor. How will you as a person cross the line into a different culture? Will you even understand why this new culture cares that you change? Will you understand why they care enough to create boundaries, barriers, laws, policies? How will you introduce yourself into that culture? How will you take the next step of participating in that culture? Through the contracting process a dialogue develops between the staff person and the participant. Hopefully, clarity on both sides is the result.

The new culture is the non-street world. Once a person decides to enter the non-street world there is a courting process. The need or will to survive exists just as strongly in the non-street world as on the street. Boundaries and barriers are often as rigid, if not more so, off the street as on the street. The starting point for the street person is often found in a statement, "I choose to be where I am, because I choose not to be where I was."

When young people begin to take the steps off the street, they not only walk through *the back door,* they walk into the non-street world where there are pre-defined behavioral expectations. The non-street world has its own authority structure to ensure that these expectations are met. Many participants fail the very minute they walk in a 'non-street door'. The street person often walks in the wrong way, looks wrong, acts wrong... without even knowing it. A non-street person will perceive their values to have been violated once their space has been encroached upon. When this happens it is hard for a street person to get a fresh start. The participant who chooses to get off the street can compare his or her life to a game of bumper pool. Once the ball goes into the bumpers it begins to bump back and forth until it finally gets out. If an individual is successful, they may not get bumped around too much. If not, they will continue to hit one bumper after another.

Whose responsibility is it that young people turn to the street?

A superficial statement can be made saying that it is the young *person* who is as fault. They *are* rebellious, they *are* aggressive, they *run* away or they just can *not* live at home. As mentioned previously, 1988, 1989 and 1990 data on the youth coming to *the back door* reveals that over 90% of the young people were placed within the child welfare system by the age of 5. When placed into this system, they were removed from what is commonly called "normal" development. They are now in a state of crisis and may remain there for a very long time.

Social welfare receives a great deal of criticism when it comes to discussing the foster care system. The context must be understood. There are many good foster parents. There are many good adoption experiences, there are also those situations that don't work. The average participant at *the back door* was in an experience that did not work. When *the back door* first began, stories were told of how the young person had been placed in a foster care home, then became a ward of the province. As they became a ward of the province they often got moved by the judicial process through the legal system.

Lets assume that the legal system really does care and that it did the best it could. The question needs to be asked, was the juvenile system put in place to replace parenting? Was the juvenile system put in place to nurture the emotional and physical well-being of each child in their custody. One must ask, is that even possible? Whose responsibility is it when young people, by the time they are fourteen years of age, have spent only a year or two out of the first fourteen years of their life in a "*normal*" family situation. It is impossible to believe that when a young person is placed in and out of many homes, and then in and out of the juvenile system or social welfare system that normal human development will happen. Now consider the reality experienced by the young person placed in the custody of child welfare because their home is not normal and may be very dysfunctional. A lot of past emotions and life experiences will block the process which would typically prepare one for "normal" matriculation into the non-street world.

When young people do not participate in a supportive home situation, it is "normal" to build up attitudes, place emphases on survival skills, and nurture anger. Street youth look at things differently. They talk differently, they have different words, they have different ways of expressing themselves, they have different expectations or lack of expectations for other members of the family. If they haven't had regular school experiences these young people will have different expectations for the roles of the teachers, principals, other students, and parents who come into the classroom.

When we begin to work with someone who chooses to get off the street, we can't start at the same point as someone who has been raised in a "normal environment". *Normal doesn't exist.* On the contrary, normal is the totally opposite scenario. There has not been a nurturing experience. There was not likely cuddling as an infant. Often the child did not have a bed or a home to claim as their own. They may not have had the opportunity to

26

run to a grandparent or an uncle or an aunt and be lovingly caressed or held in a way that brings wholeness to their life. That becomes the sought after situation.

When this young person goes into the non-street world and begins to relate to non-street people, it is very common for someone from the non-street world to say, "Why are you doing that? Why are you thinking that way? Grow up! Act differently. There is a harshness that comes with the non-street world. Even if the non-street person doesn't intend any negativism, the street person has been on the bottom so long they will automatically interpret whatever is being said as 'how wrong they are or have been'. The perceived harshness has a tendency to push a young person away from the non-street world and toward the street. It is then on the street that a street person can at least have a sense of camaraderie with other rejected people.

The human ability to survive nourishes a personal sense of power saying, "I can run away". Many times they do. They run from situation to situation to situation, without building relationships, without being nurtured, without being part of a true community of people. Although often used, the word community is a misnomer in the context of the street. The community that is built is based on what one person can take from another. Street people survive by taking advantage of each other. "I will give to you only so long as I can survive with you as part of my life." This is a crucial, significant statement, when looking at any subculture, especially the subculture of the street.

When looking at the philosophy of *the back door*, we have chosen to say that what is on the street is not part of *the back door* experiment. *The back door* represents the non-street world. We intentionally are not trying to delve into the nature of the street but rather create a touch point of departure from the street into the non-street world.

Counseling and therapy have become a part of the expectations of the non-street world. When a person needs counseling or therapy, it is not the work of *the back door*. It is the mandate of *the back door* to help create a way for a person to have a safe place, legal income and legal entry points into survivable subcultures of the non-street world. It cannot be ignored that the life situation of a participant on the street affects the difficulty of the participant's experience of getting off the street.

Who would pay for the work of *the back door*?

We started out with an understanding that we would go to the government for one third of the funding. We would go to the individuals for donations for one third of the funding. Finally we would go to the business and corporate sector for one third of the funding. The experiment was to go to these different sectors and ascertain their responses.

At the time *the back door* was starting, the Premier of the Province of Alberta, a number of the ministers on cabinet, and local politicians were all professing the need for government and community to work together. Due to my work with the Food Bank, I was in conversation with a number of these people over those same years. Time and again the statement was made: "we need to work together".

In starting *the back door* this became as much an experiment of testing the words of non-street people as it was the testing of words of street people. An assumption was made that working together meant that a project such as *the back door* could approach various sources for funding and other needs or at least that there would be an avenue to be heard.

The plan was discussed with various politicians. The funding strategy of one third, one third, and one third interested those politicians to whom it was presented. They sent us to the structures and the bureaucracies in place. We found out that the bureaucracy did not have a way to dialogue with politicians. Both sides, it seemed, were forced into adversarial roles. The politicians in a number of cases had to create their own power base to deal with the bureaucrats. Our experience was that the politicians were not in control of the government. Rather, the bureaucrats seemed to be in control of how the government worked once political mandates were set. The whole process was dysfunctional. Politicians could often be heard to say, "what you must understand is that we have discussed this with the bureaucracy. Ultimately the people who are in leadership were here before we got here, and will be here after we leave. At best we can only hope to influence and make moderate changes."

The political system does not work well when politicians perceive themselves as having a mandate to "fix" or to change the direction of society. We found that the bureaucratic process was much like the street. It was based on a hierarchical authority structure. The individuals who are at the top of the hierarchy made the decisions and 'sent memos' to the people in their systems. The workers on the lower rungs were scurrying around with so much work that staff had become paranoid over losing their jobs if they didn't jump high enough or fast enough. Staff were being burned out in the process.

Obtaining funding from community sources has its own challenges. Our experience at the Food Bank was that people would say, "We will give you money, but you can only buy food with this money. You cannot pay for staffing, you cannot pay for the trucks, you cannot pay for the delivery costs and fuel." It took almost five years before people were willing to listen to the fact that drivers had to be paid.

The same kind of experience developed at *the back door*. We went to the public and asked for donations to help get young people off the street. People questioned why we were asking for money to do this, "Don't you understand, that's the government's role?" We learned quickly that people were not interested in helping to cover operational costs. The first year we depended totally on the anonymous foundation. The second year we depended less on it. We finally got approval for government funding for a third of our costs which could be put towards administrative and operational costs.

Our next step was to go to the corporate, business and service club sectors. We asked them to pick up the costs of the bonuses for the participants. The anonymous foundation covered the cost of the bonuses for the entirety of the second year. Service clubs began coming aboard in the third year. By the end of the third year with commitment from government for the first third, the foundation for the second third, and service clubs working towards the third part it seemed as if we were well on our way.

A redirection of government funding eventually led to major cuts in both education and health care. This sent ripples through the plan, impacting all sources of giving to *the back door*. By the time we got into the fourth and the fifth years there was an epidemic of donor cuts. It seemed as if everyone was saying that they were going to change their procedures. The whole thing began to unravel and funding processes were in chaos. The survival mode had hit everywhere. "Don't you understand? We can only give so much. What we have is already allotted for." *the back door* had to change or die.

Does a safety net exist or should this concept be reinvented?

It was at this time that we began to raise the question of "who are we?" Are we a part of the safety net or are we only a community based charity?

Revenue Canada identified us as a rescue project, one that rescues people from the street such as soup kitchens, drop-in centres, mission programs and so on. As such, in their eyes we were not part of the social safety net. Standing with the participants, it was as if we were on the outside looking in. We were on the fringe of the social safety net. Yet, as we look at the program of *the back door*, we see the many times that we have dealt with circumstances pertaining to the social safety net.

We have been defined as working on the cutting edge of the charitable programs supposedly guaranteeing the social safety net. We work daily with individuals who constantly fall through the cracks of these charitable and social programs. For instance, the Canadian Job Strategy had programs which addressed many of the things we ended up doing. Yet, they too refused to help us because we were too broad in our focus.

It seemed that each time we approached a government department, its mandate was so narrow that it was not able to work with another department, let alone with us. Such concerns as housing, education, job readiness, and health all came under different mandates. Funding was offered on a "per instance" basis. All of these programs demanded that there be what is called a "sit down" or "bums-in-seat" component. This requires that people come in, sit down in a classroom, and begin to learn. In our experience this component is unsatisfactory. It is assumed that people like our participants have some form of legal income to support themselves while they are in a program. It is assumed that they have a safe place to sleep, and supportive people to help make their lives work. They don't. Time and again our participants were excluded from participating in various programs because no support network was in place. Even if secure structures could be put in place, many of our participants have been deemed to be "behavioral problems" within these structures. If a participant could qualify, it would be very difficult for them to actually *stay* in the program.

This is not an excuse to justify bad behavior. Yet it must be recognized that by the time these youth get to us they have had their lives altered and redirected due to failures in the child welfare system, the criminal justice system, the educational system, and a dysfunctional home life. These words are not excuses, they are realities.

The ability of a participant to cooperate, the values and skills necessary to succeed are just not there. A learning curve has to be created by and for each of the participants. It must be remembered that unless a person is totally removed from the street (including those things which prompt street instincts), they may sit eight hours in some training environment but he/she will spend the remaining sixteen hours per day back on the street.

31

What is learned off the street will not be reinforced back on the street.

Is the concept of a social safety net even relevant to the person coming off the street? At *the back door* we have found the concept of a "buffer zone" more appropriate. Whenever a street person is participating in some funded project they are lifted up to the safety net. When the program is over they are often dropped back on the street. A buffer zone is necessary.

Without this buffer zone street people will go on surviving. They will participate in an alternative economy not by choice but by necessity. Just as the non-street person finds motivation when there is personal economic security the street person turns to the same motivating forces. Drug money, prostitution, crime are all acceptable ways to gain an income on the street.

Education: Is the approach all it's cracked up to be?

Education is deemed to have value in our society. It has value because the reward has often been better jobs for those who participate. Schools supposedly create better people and stronger values. Education itself is seen as some kind of deliverer of the necessary tools to survive.

Most of the participants of *the back door* really never got acclimated to an educational system or an academic way of thinking. This is a learned process. Participants have been labeled as behavioral problems. They seemingly were standing outside of the education system's processes.

How the participant fits, or does not fit, in the education system can be better understood when we begin to study some of the sparse research concerning high school drop outs. The minutes of the Canadian Senate going back into the 1940's say that "approximately thirty percent of the young people will not fit into the educational system." While it may not have been intentional, our society has allowed this thirty percent to consistently drop out. We have gotten used to it. This reflects not only the broken-ness in the system but a flaw in the evaluative process. Individuals who do not finish school or do not fit in the education system do not get rewarded. It cannot be ignored however, that these same young people are learning outside of an "accredited" educational process. A new reality is now hitting us. Our society is increasingly failing to educate people for changing job markets. We are asking the question "what are we now going to do when we 'educate' a total generation of young people to unemployability?" For many the jobs are not there or jobs are there, but people are not prepared for the jobs which do exist. Unless education can coordinate with emerging markets in some fashion this problem will continue. Many people are ending up in entry level jobs just to survive. Inflexibility of both the system and people in the educational system is leading to an economic collision.

This raises another issue for *the back door*. The competition for the entry level jobs is getting more and more complex. Summer students who are in the school system often get the entry level work. With more and more young people being left out of the educational process there are fewer entry level jobs available for them. Therefore with less entry level jobs available there become fewer and fewer port-holes of departure from the street. A job is imperative if a person is to get off the street.

It gets more complicated because drugs, alcohol and the behavioral problems the street person brings with them usually push them away from access to grants and training programs. Hence the route to the safety net has yet one more gaping hole.

The education system must also be looked at to see if it has elements which are deterrents to maintaining a safety net. Traditional education is the way extolled to guarantee a better and more successful life. Education envisions a child starting in kindergarten or in preschool. The child goes on to grade one, grade two, grade three, and grade four with an understanding that children will have automatic 'normal' growth patterns. Individuals

33

who are raised in housing projects, broken homes, child welfare or other interrupted processes do not have these 'normal' processes to build on. In poverty, many of the 'normal' developmental patterns are interrupted. Therefore, it must be understood that the emotional and psychological development of young people who have ended up on the street will also be interrupted. Their life experience does not fit the patterns nurtured in the education system. An interesting parallel is now developing at various socio-economic levels. Pressures caused by work and/or lifestyle issues are creating similar interruptions for other children. At the same time the educational system is being affected by this phenomenon. The safety net continues to be stressed. As service providers have more and more credentials, the costs of keeping these providers within the system begin to jeopardize the very existence of the safety net.

It goes deeper than an economic issue. Teachers, support workers and others are increasingly faced with issues in the classroom that go beyond academics - dysfunctional home environments, attention deficit disorder and so on. Often these are beyond the teachers ability to manage. It is not uncommon for the teachers or other school workers to lose interest in relating to the social problems a child brings with them. Indeed, it is often written out of the school's job descriptions. Once again the tension between education and child welfare comes to the forefront interrupting the educational process that should be available to everyone.

The 'Buffer-Zone': a byproduct of holes in the safety-net!

There are young people who go into the school system who do not think in, what are defined as, rational thought patterns. They are labeled as irrational thinkers. The street world is defined as irrational because it just does not follow the same patterns of the non-street world. It just does not behave in acceptable ways for the non-street world. On the contrary, the street is extremely rational. It is very predictable.

Another consideration is the situation of the person who is a 'gifted person' and bored with traditional ways of thinking. They do not fit an education system designed to work with what is defined as the 'average student' or the student who will adapt to the expectations of the system. Teachers, vice principals, principals, and school boards say they do not have the funds to deal with students one-on-one to accommodate such special scenarios.

Like the gifted students many of the participants of *the back door* have in the past needed this one-on-one attention. Because of this, at *the back door* we describe what we do as participating in a buffer zone. The participant falls through the net into this zone and then climbs out of it. This is a pattern. It is a very consistent pattern, arising out of very rational behavior.

At *the back door* we became aware of a conflict which ultimately created a dilemma that we did not want to accept. We really did want to believe in the role of government funding a safety net. It was our experience that as young people came to us, if they perceived we were funded by government, there was an attitude of entitlement. "You owe us that." At one point we were asking government for help. When we got that help it was counter-productive to the participant. Eventually participants learned how to care where funding and support came from. If the funds came from donations or our own funding projects, the participants saw that sometimes the funds came and sometimes they did not come. The participants developed an understanding that they were not alone in this walk off the street. Instead of expecting it, they were hopeful that the money would be there. Once they began to hope the money was there they also began to take more ownership around the money that was available. We learned something about ourselves. The closer we were to walking the thin line of survival, the closer we were to our participants coming to understand that they too can survive if only for this day.

This led to further conflict. How fair is it for an agency to constantly live on survival's edge? If we talk about asking participants to join an upwardly mobile society, how can we justify asking staff to sacrifice everything so others can survive? The answer is found in the life and work of Mother Theresa. She made the choice to work among the poor. She took a vow of poverty but still found her support in a wealthy community. She did not pay her own hospital bills, nor did she pay for her ongoing education. She received these things because she participated in a very supportive community. This illustrates for us that it has to be okay to work toward the creation of yet another sub-system which will be there not only for the participants but for the staff and volunteers as well.

Concepts too easily taken for granted: Traditional thinking needs to be challenged

More and more young people are ending up on the streets. Ten years ago when we first began to talk about the crisis many refused to acknowledge its existence. Today major cities all across Canada are speaking of the thousands of young people on Canadian streets. This is very serious scenario; the bottom of the bottom. Just as people would respond to a natural disaster or military intervention, society should also respond to this crisis.

Societal shifts happen. Economic shifts happen. Decisions are taken or made by government, corporations, highway departments, school administrators, and religious leaders. When they do, the decision makers are like the wheels of a clock. They move ponderously slow. The big wheels often forget how much faster the small wheels have to work just to survive. The street person is often that tiny wheel that has so often gone unnoticed. In light of this, traditional roles need to be questioned.

Traditional understanding needs to be challenged: the poor you _will_ have with you always.

As technological shifts continue, people unable to participate in the shift drop out of the job market. People will be out of work. The economy has shifted away from non-skilled employment. When this happens, young people are the first to run. Parents often say to their kids, "go where the jobs are". When young people leave home, they go looking for jobs. Cities like Calgary boast of economic growth in jobs. Politicians travel the countryside extolling the virtues of economic growth and opportunity. These same politicians' words broadcast around the world. Young people who are poor watch television. They hear these words and come running hoping to find the proverbial land of milk and honey.

Calgary, like other cities, did not and does not plan ahead when it concerns the poor. Entry level housing, health care facilities, community based schools with social support systems did not exist for youth ten years ago when *the back door* started. In fact, very little has changed. It is true we have more programs in Calgary for street youth now than ever before, but it is also true these programs exist on the street and, for the most part, turn people back to the street after having offered some form of service.

While social planning councils talk about preparing for bringing in new jobs or bringing in new industry, there is an absence of planning for the bottom or entry level rungs of society. Therefore, when money is invested in highly paid and skilled jobs, those people who don't have a higher education, or those who don't fit into the high end circles do not have services built for them. Most longer term planning does not cover the full spectrum of society.

Short-term plans have brought long-term fallout. Health, education, court, police, jailing and imprisonment costs, as well as deterioration of community are often ignored. Someone will eventually have to pick up the pieces.

When we first started *the back door* there were those in the Calgary Police Department who said that if a young person came to Calgary without having a social support network to tie into, it would take 30 days or less for that young person to end up on the street. They will connect with the street because the street becomes its own form of alternative support system. Why are young people on the street? Not just because of brokenness in their own lives but because the society they are entering into is also broken. Entry level ports are perceived as being inaccessible.

Young peoples lives are broken. Young people do end up on the street. It isn't just the failure of the smaller rural communities to cope with our industrial developments which is at issue. Families often move into cities without a support base. Their young people often end up on the street. They become a cost to the system.

In Calgary, we will graduate thousands of young people from high school each year. We do not have entry level housing for them when they leave home. Even if we ignore the question of street youth, young people find themselves having to double up, triple up, quadruple up in apartments where landlords don't want them. They end up being kicked out. There is not enough entry level housing available for the non-street, let alone the street.

Most of the young people on the streets of Calgary are not Calgarians, just as most of the young people in Toronto or any other city are not native to the city where they are. Youth are transient. They live as part of an alternative culture. This culture has been with us since the beginning of time. It only makes sense that it be recognized for what it is. To know it is there, and will probably always be there, does not give permission to ignore it. In fact if it is possible to learn from it, ways can be created so that it doesn't have to keep on getting worse. *To have the poor with you*, is an invitation for society to respond to this crisis, not to 'baptize' it as acceptable.

Money really isn't the only issue

When *the back door* began, we started with a perspective that money was not the only issue. If the issue of young people getting off the street, in fact never going on the street, is to be addressed, it will take the total participation of the whole community. A dialogue including all parts of society needs to recognize not only the presence of an overall culture but the presence of many subcultures.

We began *the back door* with a goal to help young people get off the street. The second part of our mandate was to help non-street people to understand just how they can help, how they can participate in the process of getting a young person off the street. That is why the initial proposal to develop *the back door* was developed in such a way that the board of education, the social welfare people, the various representatives of government, social clubs, service clubs, churches, community people, and all of the people who were involved in the matter were invited into the original discussion. What we discovered along the way was that people were quite interested in discussing the issue. They did not seem to be interested in getting behind the matter to the point of doing something about it. There were just so many agendas that it was hard to get anything accomplished.

When thinking about who the potential volunteers are and who wants to help, one must look at the concept of volunteering. Why is it that people volunteer? In a number of cases, people volunteer to feel better, so they can commit themselves to a better and healthier lifestyle. There is a tension between doing volunteer work for personal gratification and/or actually being a servant to society. This was true at *the back door* as well. If *the back door* is going to ask people to volunteer, are these volunteer hours set up to the benefit of the volunteer or to the benefit of the street person?

the back door's history with volunteers started out somewhat speckled. At first we felt *manipulated* by volunteer demands. In time this changed. With the introduction of a volunteer contract it could be clarified not only why a volunteer was coming, but very specifically, for what task. The volunteer understood for him/herself why they had come. An unexpected surprise developed. We now see individuals coming with a clear understanding of what we are about. We also see businesses, service clubs, social groups, church groups putting aside their agendas and just being helpful.

For *the back door* to be really successful, funds need to be channeled into diverse activities that support the whole person including recreation, sports, hobbies, and many areas familiar to the lifestyles of persons not on the street. Young people need things to do in a creative learning participatory environment to displace unproductive down time. These things, however, cannot replace the need to find a safe place to live, a way to feed oneself and a way for a person to learn how to care for him or herself. The non-street person will need to use their ability to make the market work for others as well as themselves.

The volunteer needs to remember the tremendous economic differences between themselves and the street. The change for someone coming from the street is no different than for someone coming from a foreign country and settling in Canada. In fact, it may even be more difficult because the average street person now dresses better, has more soup kitchens to go to and is often looked at as not needing help in the support structures.

Getting off the street none-the-less still costs money

Learning how to survive economically is a part of the process of getting off the street. How does a person pay for rent? How does a person pay for food? How does a person pay for utilities or clean clothing so they can actually fit into the non-street world? These are all crucial issues when thinking about the role of the community.

Economically, society traditionally looks at three classes of people: the upper class, the middle class and the lower class. At *the back door*, we had to emphasize 10 classes of people. This reflects multiple layers in each class with attention needing to be paid to specific transitional issues. The upper upper class, the middle upper class, the lower upper class, and then the upper middle class, the middle middle class, the lower middle class, and then the upper lower class, the middle lower class, and finally the lower class. There is another category, the people who find themselves outside of connecting points with the non-street world. They are the class-less society. They create their own alternative society. Often this society is based on a power base rather than on economics. The street itself reflects this alternative society.

Many in the non-street world want to think that the street world does not exist. It does exist. Just as in the Soviet Block countries, an alternative economic community had developed the street exists with its own economy. It has its own structure. It has its own economic policies. It has its own policing department. It has its own educational institutions. It has its own health care. It has all of these things. Unfortunately, they do not exist for the betterment of the street person. The street is an alternative society based on violence and survival first.

If a person is going to leave that world, they will need to have a way to enter into employment and educational options which will allow them to afford the non-street world. If this does not happen then there is no reason for the street person to leave the street behind.

Getting off the street is an immigration process

We recognize the street as its own culture. If a person who has been raised in that culture moves to the non-street world they are entering a new culture. It can be paralleled to an immigration process.

It should not be ignored that when someone moves from the east coast to the west coast of Canada they are going through significant cultural change. In fact, the number one highway is the main conduit for Canadian immigration. Thousands of young people every day traverse from city to city. These changes should be recognized as immigration patterns.

When we first started *the back door*, Alberta Career Development & Employment had a program for new immigrants, people coming from other countries. When we assessed that program, we found it to be a very good program if it could be adapted to the street world. The questions needing to be answered were all included. The government people who created that program had done a very good job of listing the needs, the requirements for human development, the mental health questions, and all of the other concerns which needed to be addressed for a new immigrant to integrate into this new Canadian culture.

At *the back door*, we attempted to go to the government with this question: "Would you be willing to recognize the street as an alternative culture?" Because the young person on the street is considered a Canadian, the government could not make that crossover. We attempted to argue for the indigenous nature of each of the communities across Canada. We attempted to recognize the multiple cultures in Calgary. Each of these cultures bring with them various aspects of surviving. Therefore, there needed to be a multi-cultural dialogue which included the subculture of the street. This was not being heard.

One of the crucial things we attempted to address was the role of mental health as a supportive part of identifying the need to nurture the individual. The average person who goes to school has his or her schooling subsidized by the tax system. The average person who goes for a medical examination has his or her medical care subsidized by the tax system. The average person entering into a therapeutic process has this subsidized by taxes. If a person goes to jail, they have their survival subsidized by taxes. If they are in jail and enrolled in an education course, it is subsidized by a taxes. Any mental health or personal training component within the incarceration process is also subsidized by a taxes.

Once a person is taken out of that tax-based support system, as when coming out of the jail system, he or she may be put on the street at 6:00 am on a Sunday morning. The support stops. They could be told to show up for court dates, therapy, this or that and make sure to stay out of trouble. They have just been put on the street. How are they going to stay out of trouble? If there is not a single connection to a support system how is that person going to survive? How is a person going to make that transition back into society?

At *the back door*, we simply start by asking the young person "So what is the most imminent crisis you are facing at this moment?" That becomes step one. "What is the next most imminent crisis you are facing?" That becomes step two.

At *the back door*, we acknowledge the need to address *crisis* as a state of being. It is not only surviving; it is also an all encompassing way of thinking. The non-street world requires long-term planning, whereas the street world operates from a crisis mentality which says that in any given hour of any given day there will be a new variable introduced because the street world is in a constant state of conflict.

The non-street world is the dominant culture. In Canada the street world is a minority subculture within the overall culture. Before asking a young person to leave the street world, *the back door's* role is to facilitate an understanding of how many roadblocks there are in the way of entering that world. Non-street expectations become powerful barriers to the street person. The street person has to ask: do they even want to join the non-street?

This is no longer only a social question. It is an economic question as well. If the street culture is allowed to continue, it will grow as an alternative culture. There eventually will be, as there are in third world countries all around the world, a clashing of the cultures, which moves the non-street world to say that it needs a more powerful police force. A police force to police a society costs money. But more than that, it costs freedom. When a society gives permission for a police society to develop, personal freedom is ultimately at risk. The very things which non-street people work hard to maintain and develop, (i.e., that which is perceived to be a high standard in everything for a better quality of life) is also lost.

It is the perception of *the back door*, that *the back door* process represents venture capital. It represents a way to invest in one person at a time. As these people get off the street, history tells us that they assume very traditional non-street lives. They have become butchers, cooks, dry wallers, cribbers, security guards, painters, janitors, carpet cleaners, and the occasional scholar!

The message of *the back door* is that it's okay to want to have good educational services. It is okay to want to have good medical services. It is okay to want to have good employment services. However, while all of these things are okay, it's important that the non-street world understands that options are to be guaranteed so that all people can access the services that would be potentially provided.

the back door would not lobby for a guaranteed income. *the back door* argues for a guaranteed way for people to access the services that are being offered. These services enable an individual to obtain a fair income. *the back door* does not lobby for low income housing. *the back door* argues for a way for all people to enter the housing market so that eventually all people can make their own choices in housing. *the back door* does not lobby for specialized educational systems. *the back door* argues that the educational system allows for people, whoever they are, to get an education. *the back door* argues that an integrative process be created in the system so that all peoples have entry points to access those processes necessary to human survival.

In December 1989 these words were written for The Canadian Institute of Planners' Journal:

> If there are to be changes in social planning, street people will need to feel ownership in matters affecting their own lives. Street people must see alternatives which include them as participants in the planning process, not just clients to be considered. Street people must be able to envision how attempting to move into mainline society is of benefit to them.

Planning needs to include the transition time necessary for the planners and street culture to understand each other. To only move people from one part of the city to another part of the city is not a solution. One must look at the welfare of the whole community. Social planning includes the intentional design by a community of people to seek the welfare of the whole community. Issues which were once identified as only street concerns are now becoming topics of conversation everywhere. A solution which does not include the street will only be sabotaged because the source of social problems will go ignored and will only reoccur in another setting. If the reasons for people being on the street and what happens to people when changes to the community are made are not considered, social planning will continue to be a cyclical event. Planners will continue to address the same issues over and over again. The solution must include those who will be affected by the decision making process.

Variables - the experiment began: an "introduction to a life of variables"

Words as a part of the experiment

When we were developing *the back door*, people would ask us what *the back door* was. We found that when we talked about *the back door* as a project, as if it were something, an entity, an existence, we found that people didn't pay that much attention to us or to our words. It was, "Oh, yes, it's just another project."

We discovered that each group of people had their own vocabulary. What meant something to one group often had a different meaning to another group. Sometimes it was a slight variation, other times the difference was quite significant. 'Homeless' was one of these words. If a person had a roof over their head they were not considered homeless by some, even if this was for only one night. In some situations 'homeless' was given as a label to someone who had no permanent residence. Many people just could not believe that any one could be homeless.

In order to enter school, or be counted for the census, or qualify for health care, a person needed a permanent address. The words "permanent address" became an instant barrier to a person's participation. This term became the ultimate qualifier or disqualifier for accessing opportunities or services.

The word 'experiment' gave us freedom to develop and become something before we were pigeon-holed. When we introduced *the back door* as an "experiment", then people paid attention to it, asked questions about who we were, what we were doing, what we hoped the results would be and what we thought the results were becoming. They were actually more involved in what might happen. We took their cue and we decided that throughout the initial steps of *the back door*, we would use the word experiment on a consistent basis. *the back door* is an experiment. It is an experiment to determine what the cost is to move someone off the street. Those words then helped us to take a look at some very key thoughts and issues.

Location as a part of the experiment.

the back door started in January 1988, the same year the Olympics came to Calgary and preparation actually commenced mid 1987. This meant there was very little property available. Time and again we went to various locations. We thought we had the places rented. There was a handshake agreement. Before I came back with money in hand the place was gone. We lost place after place because of people who were coming into Calgary just to do business during the Olympics. In many cases these people offered more money to rent buildings for a short time than we could afford for a full year.

This is an important factor when one looks at how any kind of project such as *the back door* gets started. If the real estate market has a high demand, then considering the kind of project *the back door* is and the population we work with, there is very little interest in renting to people like us.

46

We ended up in a former drugstore in a small Macleod Trail strip mall that had been sitting empty for quite a while. It had been vandalized considerably. We were able to go into it for a dollar per square foot, which was a phenomenal price. It came with strings attached. If given a 30 day notice we were out. We could not assume a long-term lease. The building ownership was being settled in court. We cleaned the place out and made it livable. We found that it was a very good location. The participants were able to take the Light Rail Transit (LRT), and it was just a short walk from the train station to the office building. It worked. Within 10 months the landlord came to us and said that the building was now sold. The new owners gave us a letter saying that the rent would be in the vicinity of $15 to $16 per square foot, plus operating expenses.

Our second location was only about a block and a half away from our first location. It too, was on both Macleod Trail and the LRT line. Participants had to walk up a hill, a total of five to six blocks to get to the office. Until recently, we were always located a minimum of 90 blocks outside of the downtown core. People would ask us the question, "How come you're located so far from the downtown? Street people don't want to go out there." We would simply say, "We're doing an experiment and part of this experiment is to find out what effect being outside the downtown core has on the lives of young street people." We found the location affected the participants in different ways. As participants were going out of the downtown they were influenced by the different environments, situations, and people they encountered. We also found that being that far from the downtown became a safety factor. Drug dealers, pimps and others who had a reason to give chase, get even, or take something from a participant, did not follow them out of the downtown core. This allowed the participant to begin the process of breaking away from the street.

As a result of the first location we got our name: *the back door*. The only way to get into the building was to walk completely around the shopping centre and go in through the back door. People would call us and we would say, "Come around to the back door." As we kept saying that, it wasn't long before people started calling us *'the back door'*. "Just go to the back door." The name stuck and we registered it that way.

An interesting thing about the name is that it is safe for the street. On the street a back door was often a place of business. It was a place through which people could escape. It was a place to which people could run away from potential harm. On the other hand, many non-street people didn't like the name. It conjured up negative images and left people often wondering just what we were doing. They said, "Why don't you change the name?" However, *'the back door'* stuck.

During the first years it was impressed upon us that being outside of the downtown core was absolutely imperative. The participants, whether they rode the bus, or the LRT, were moving to a whole new starting point. That became very important because it caused the participant to psychologically change their mind set. As they were riding the public transportation or sometimes walking out to the location, they would have to enter a different world: a world of business; a world of merchandising; a world where people were working. They were going to a place of business.

the back door opens at eight o'clock in the morning and stays open until five o'clock in the afternoon, daytime business hours. That doesn't mean we don't keep the doors open after that, but we have always tried to run *the back door* as if it were a business. At times, once the participants got jobs, our staff would actually go to the participant's place of work to contract. This was done by appointment. Once again the business location encouraged business behavior. This helped to bring both authenticity and accountability to their story. Participants did not ask us to contract in other locations unless they were really serious. That seriousness was very important to us.

Another benefit to being outside the downtown core was that it allowed some of the participants to go to a social service office away from a very parasitic street environment. If a participant needed to buy steel-toed boots or qualify for a damage deposit and they went to a social service office away from the downtown, other street people would not be waiting for them as they came out the door.

All too often the participant experienced the street phenomenon 'what's yours is mine'. If the participant were identified as potentially getting money, a voucher or anything deemed to be of value, the law of the street would cause the participant to become a target. Becoming a target meant that if money were owed for any reason it was now to be collected. Unfortunately that experience was duplicated many times. It did not have to be just at social services. It might be at a soup kitchen, or any other place where the street network could identify someone. Once a participant was identified by the street network, if they did not "cough up..." they would be in trouble with the street. There was too much street stuff going on that participants could easily reconnect with or have connected with them. It was not our goal to tell a participant what they could or could not do. It was our goal to attempt to create space in such a way that the participant had to think about what and why they were doing what they were doing.

The street serves as a training ground: a minor league for gangs as these gangs attempted to get a foothold in Calgary. Many of the young people who came to *the back door* would be seen as runners, as people who were on the periphery, people who were making just small amounts of money to survive. The street is a seed bed for the criminal element. You can't deal drugs without being involved with the criminal world. By being located that far out of the downtown core many of the participants disconnected from the communication process of the street. There was a need to literally build a network totally outside of the downtown core. The presence of *the back door* in a commercial zone, in an area far outside residential communities which had been identified as high drug use areas and areas of high criminal activity, allowed the participants an alternative starting point. It was/is not uncommon for a participant from *the back door* to not want to go back downtown.

History repeated itself in that the rent on Macleod Trail once again became too high for us. We began our search to find a new home. In addition to the cost of rent we faced an ethical quandary. It was becoming painfully obvious that as long as we were in an office building other potential tenants did not want to come into the building. An interesting thing happened. When we left that building, it wasn't days before the entire office building was rented. Before that, almost one third of it sat empty. Was the vacancy rate affected by the presence of *the back door* or not? All I can tell you is that within days, a building that had close to 20,000 square feet of empty space, was all of a sudden totally rented. In some sense it can perhaps be attributed to a change in the market. In another sense it cannot.

We attempted to find another location outside the downtown core in the Chinook area. This would be no more than a mile away from where we were on Heritage and Macleod Trail while still being on the LRT line. We found a building. We sublet that building and planned to move in during the month of December '97. The owner of that building who apparently lived outside Calgary was out of town when the agreement was reached. She came into my office, and very carefully said that they would not sublet that building to us, even if they had to take us to court and even though the property manager had signed the lease. That person would not give approval for us to be there.

This person said they had rented property to a project dealing with street people previously and their property had been severely abused. We said we had no problem going to our past landlords to prove that we were very good tenants. In fact, our present landlord said that we were an exceptionally good tenant. The building was not destroyed in any way. This did not persuade the prospective landlord. No, we could not move into that building. Rather than fight, we tore up the lease. They gave us back the cheque for our deposit and we went in search of another location.

At present *the back door* is located just outside of the downtown core. We're only twenty-five blocks from the center of the downtown. For us, this is far too close to the downtown. We've been here for two years and we're experiencing other street people showing up on the periphery. They wait on the property for our participants to come out of the building which is located in a community that has been known for street related behaviors. While we believe this is a very nice building to work out of it is not a safe location for our participants. We are again looking for another location. We hope this new location will be separated by natural boundaries from the downtown so the participants will be in a community that is disassociated from the street culture.

Staffing as part of the experiment

Staffing became a very interesting, dilemma. Who should be the people making up the staff? How much should they get paid? What role would volunteers play?

When we began *the back door* we interviewed a number of applicants with the goal of developing a multi-disciplinary team made up of a social worker, a teacher, a business person and one other person. This other person had to be a woman in a role of authority. We needed to identify philosophically with the issue of poverty as a matriarchal culture. Women, structurally have an extremely important presence in poverty. Number one, they are present. It is usually the mother, the aunt, or the grandmother who is the key family member present. Secondly, they are often the only voice of authority consistently there. Thirdly, they participate in a dialogue within their community. No one will survive in the ghetto or the projects without some form of network. To survive, this informal network has to exist. Fourthly, not to belabor the point, but women are available and the entanglements of being the responsible person to raise a family and participate in the network often precludes such women from leaving and climbing the economic ladder even if they could. It was then taken as a given that a woman in an authority role would be necessary at *the back door*.

In our case Marilyn Dyck took on this role when she became the office manager. She had a gentle way of saying things to participants after they had finished their contracting. As she was giving someone their $15 bonus they were very open to talk to her and to listen as well. The contracting process was and is a team process. Continual reaffirmation with meaningful dialogue remains very important.

It was believed that this team of a social worker, a school teacher, and a business person would be able to work together because they could represent their own area of expertise. When we first sat down in staff meetings, specific roles and philosophical postures were identified as stemming from respective professions. It wasn't long before we began to see how territorial each of these disciplines could be. Each staff person not only brought with them their own belief systems, but they also brought with them the expectations of their respected disciplines. The staff themselves were surprised by this whole process. As time went by each person began to assimilate each other's views into their thought process. It was here that the experiment faced what eventually became the first real challenge.

The person who was the school teacher refused to give bonuses. She believed there should be a measurable criteria for receiving the bonus based on a minimum wage concept. For her the bonus was $15, so it required a minimum three hours work. On the contrary the bonus had been created out of a need for clean money and trust in the participant which paralleled the role of bonuses in the corporate sector with its need for affirming workers.

The parallel between *the back door* and the corporate sector is necessary. The goal of *the back door* was to participate in an equal player concept. The aforementioned staff person gave an ultimatum. Either bonuses be restructured or no contracting would be done. An alternative ultimatum was given. This project was an experiment, an experiment by nature must adhere to its original purpose, measure the process of achieving this purpose and then draw conclusions. By changing the bonus process the experiment would not being given a fair trial. The staff person then left us.

The role of the school teacher was now gone. The person was missed but, interestingly enough, the task was not. Most of the participants coming to us could not access the school system. It was not our goal to start our own school but rather that the school teacher use her own background to help participants access the educational system. Each staff person was to use their own understanding to clarify and eventually access the necessary systems and steps which were being designed by the participants.

Shortly after the teacher left we were contacted by the Calgary Board of Education. They offered to lend us a person. This person was a soon-to-retire principal. He came on staff and did a very fine job while operating in many ways separate from the project. He never contracted with participants. He used space to set up a schooling alternative. Participants could do school work, he could grade their work and give appropriate credit for the work done. His work with us was later used by the Calgary Board of Education to set up a street school separate from *the back door*.

As time went on, our staff began to change. Most of the reason for the change dealt with finances. Each person originally hired was paid as if they were a part of their own system. During the first year, a social worker came to us from Alberta Social Services. This person was paid the same wages that they would have received if they had been working for Alberta Social Services. The wage for the school teacher was the same as the Calgary Board of Education.

The business person was hired on a different premise. This work was to be done as if it was a contract agreement. This person was available more or less as a consultant to the participants. This was again consistent with each discipline.

After the first three years we found that our financial stability was increasingly precarious. As finances became more tenuous the demands placed on us to maintain a professional environment began to strain the project. Professionals by definition needed to have an environment which upgraded their skills, encouraged them to do further education, writing or research. When we began, each staff person was allotted specific time for each of these areas. One third of their time was to be spent contracting with participants, one third was to be spent in community networking, and the final third was to be spent in personal and professional development. We found that the cost of maintaining staff was actually burdening the project as early as the second year.

Once staff began to ask for raises, vacation time, educational time, the existing budget demands did not keep up with the income of the project. We were quickly introduced to surviving the pecking order of social programming. In one case when we approached a government source we were told that we were overpaying our staff. Even though our staff person had come from their department and was paid the same wages as when that person had been a part of that department. The response was: remember you are an NGO (non government organization). It became abundantly clear that more and more time would be spent attempting to maintain and afford a professional environment. As a charity, developed from grass roots, we did not have the ability to keep up with the rising costs of living.

For the first years, the staff's willingness to wrestle with these issues allowed us to keep basically the same staff. As time went on, the nature of our staff changed. We had staff meetings which each of the staff people took turns leading. We found that people liked the participatory leadership process. It really worked well. However, when finances began to slow down, and donations weren't coming in, and the staff were asked to participate in the fund raising they would say, "but, we're professionals. We don't do those kinds of things." The question arose: if you hire professional staff who are not fund raisers how do you pay them? We were confronted with issues of defining fairness. If people were accepted as professionals in a professional role, perks and bonuses needed to be added. How could we discuss bonuses for participants and not for the staff?

As mentioned, Revenue Canada classified us as a rescue mission. They did not have a multidisciplinary category unless we were legally part of the medical or educational community. Hence it grew increasingly more difficult to present ourselves in the same way as other professionals did. This was not only true of the expectations of Revenue Canada but also of society in general. In the funding process many asked, "Are you sure that none of this money is going toward administration?" It was a very interesting dilemma we faced at that point. We found staff experiencing internal struggles around their own self worth and personal value to society. Staff had been trained to believe that self worth is tied to compensation. Hence when the economic crunch hit us, this one issue of staff compensation hit us with more power than any of the stress brought on by the participants or problems with structures and the proverbial systemic evils. We were forced to decide whether to continue with *the back door* or not. Staff stayed with us as long as we could pay wages. Ultimately a decision had to be made. Should we, would we, be able to continue *the back door*?

Throughout the first five years there was constant tension around the role of professional staff and the role of volunteers. Ultimately it was finances which decided who would be carrying the lion's share of the work. The professionals created the system that the volunteers eventually worked in. We had a handful of volunteers who had been trained in the contracting process. These people, and the two administrative persons stayed on. It was determined that since 70% of the young people were challenging the odds and succeeding then maybe we should try one more time. *the back door* continued.

Volunteers as part of the experiment

The role of volunteers in staffing *the back door* has been a very interesting part of our history. It started with volunteers working alongside staff. Staff said they were the professionals and volunteers shouldn't do the contracting. When staff asked for additional vacation time or holiday time, the question was then asked, who's going to take your place if you're not there? Inevitably, pragmatism became the definer of roles. This process was not without conflict. Yet conflict became a healer in that job descriptions and roles began to develop based on the strengths and weakness of each person.

In time, staff began to take turns in developing volunteer programming. "Just what can volunteers do?" Can they do the role of the professional, or do they stand outside of that role? A training program called "In Process" for the volunteers to learn to do contracting was then developed. Remaining staff began to train people in specific areas. As "In Process" was developed, more and more people began to come from other projects in the city for this training.

"In Process" was a series of six sessions where people trained to do contracting and learned about *the back door.* The end result was that volunteers <u>did</u> come in to do contracting.

At first, we accepted volunteers for a longer term commitment. As volunteers began to get involved with the participants, a number of volunteers were dissatisfied that participants' lives weren't changing fast enough.

An occasional volunteer would want to meet with participants after hours. It became necessary to develop a volunteer contract which included discussions and training around issues of safety and how dependency issues of the participant could actually sabotage movement away from the street. This contract identified the needs of *the back door* participants as primary. It then asked where the volunteer saw him or herself fitting in.

The struggle to define acceptable and unacceptable behavior for volunteers at times got muddy. If a participant felt they could manipulate one volunteer against another or against *the back door* it usually happened.

When this happened a participant would go to a specific volunteer because they believed they were being treated as someone special. If they were being treated as someone special, then why not special favors. The volunteer then found they couldn't keep giving to only one participant without giving to another. When this happened word got on the street *the back door* contract could be bypassed. The volunteer then became the target of other street people. When a street person felt slighted they would become angry, would come to *the back door* and would then tell staff about what was going on. What started out as good intentions by the volunteer inevitably ended otherwise.

An ongoing problem for both *the back door* and the volunteer also developed. Economics again entered the picture. Many times when people came as volunteers they were unemployed and looking for work. When income producing work did not materialize at *the back door* the volunteer had to move on.

Participant contracting as part of the experiment

In 1988, the concept was that each staff person would contract with ten participants. Participants would rotate between the staff for different types of contracting. As time went on we found that a case load scenario was not beneficial for the participants. The caseload approach created a dependency on the availability of the staff person and the relationship which was being developed. Personalities soon came into view. What if the staff person didn't like the participant? What if the participant didn't like the staff person? What if there were just personality conflicts which created communication barriers between staff and other staff or staff and participants?

The contracting process had faced yet another hurdle. In time it was discovered that when a participant could come in, pick up their contract, and contract with whomever was available, it encouraged more self ownership. Growth and personal development then shifted from a professional evaluation to a much simpler understanding for the participant. Did this contract work or not? In many cases, if the participant had had a long relationship with a social welfare system, we found it very hard to break their pattern of dependency on the system. On one occasion a participant came to my office cursing and swearing. The concern was that a certain staff person was impossible to contract with. This participant said, "You're my social worker. Do something about it!" I did. I stood up and strongly said, "if there is a social worker around here, it is you. If you are going to get off the street, you will have to learn how to talk to people like him. Your new life away from the street will be filled with people just like him."

Once the ground rules for contracting were developed, expectations for and by the participants began to settle down. In staff meetings, we could ask about the progress of each of the participants based more on participants' plans rather than the perceived expectations of the systems of welfare, education and especially potential employers.

As staff represented their disciplines they modeled a concept of having the freedom to say, "I don't know. You really need to talk to so and so about that." For instance, social workers and dock foremen typically just do not think alike. In fact staff meetings were often interrupted with words around defining what would/could be "fair" expectations to ask of a participant or employer. Staff found that as they learned about the other disciplines, it gave participants more freedom to trust their own conclusions as well. Each staff person had to answer questions about areas that they were not expert in. They found themselves deferring to the participant with, what did so and so say? How did so and so say that would conflict with this or that plan? For instance would an employer allow you the time in the middle of the day to see a social worker? Would the employer allow you to take one day or two days a week to go to school?

The whole idea of the contracting moved more toward an active form of listening and clarifying instead of giving advice. Most of the staff had been trained to be professional advice givers.

Contracting simply became: it is your life what do you want to do with it? How do you see yourself getting there, and what steps are necessary to get where you want to go? One of the first participants who came to *the back door* said he wanted to become an astronaut. He was obviously stoned as he came in the door. This person was told he was already higher than any astronaut had gone. He would need to come back tomorrow when he was sober. He then needed to look at his present life situation, identify what he had going for himself at this point in life and to build a plan toward the next step. His first step was to get the drugs out of his system and to learn to think clearly. He did just that. Ten years later he finished university. During his contracting time he was in and out of treatment. He had multiple jobs. He kept coming back. For him it worked.

The contracting process allowed participants to be included in the planning process. At *the back door* the only qualification to enter the contracting process is to say you want to get off the street. After all these years we have learned that if someone doesn't need us they will tell us so. They will wean themselves from the contract. We will accept whoever comes through the door. At first that created problems. Then it became a way of life for us. If there was a contract spot open the next person walking through the door qualified. We did not hold spots. We did not ask people to put their lives on hold just so they could be a part of *the back door*. One of the most interesting things in this entire process is that, while we declared *the back door* an experiment, over time, the need to change the contract never developed.

Variations in ways of approaching and dealing with life, are a fact of life. There are also variations in contracting approaches. Some of the staff would talk about contracting for a full month at a time, others would talk about contracting for a day at a time. In all cases, each of the participants were given the freedom to say what their plans were/are. In some cases participants had grown to the point where they could make longer term plans. Sometimes they fell back into the need to take one step at a time.

Another interesting component is the contract itself. It has developed into an interactive dialogue between the participant and the computer. By sitting at the computer, the computer holds the participant accountable to a specific thought process. This has given the participant a way to plan. The computer helps in the defogging process. When a person lives on the street or is a part of the drug culture, their brain is affected. Very specific thinking patterns develop. Off the street these patterns are believed to be irrational. On the street they may be extremely rational simply because there are so many variables constantly bombarding the participant. Because the computer is so rational, a rational planning approach is then introduced into the participant's thinking process time and again. Planning is something a person has to do all the time, even if it means simply getting a haircut, a different jacket or a pair of runners. The participants work on a plan, then they begin to see it evolve in front of his or her eyes.

An aside to this whole contracting process deals with rumblings we heard from the street. Sometime about the fourth or fifth year of the project, we began to hear the words coming back to us from the street, "Don't go to *the back door* unless you're serious about getting off the street. *the back door* has limited funds. Therefore, don't go there if all you're going to do is scam. If all you're going to do is to try to take advantage of *the back door*, don't. There are people who are serious about getting off the street, let those people go to *the back door* first."

This was an interesting development. When people first came to *the back door*, they came very specifically to try to scam for the bonus money.

It doesn't mean that people still don't scam for bonus money. Scamming is a way of life for many. (If it wasn't, there would be no need for truth in advertising laws.) Scamming is a way that people frequently rationalize their own survival and buffer zones. People move toward less and less scamming as they become more and more economically settled. The scamming process is something we cannot be afraid of. There seems to be a developmental process. For the first month, street people do not trust us. They come, they seldom take their contracting seriously. If they do take their contracting seriously, they'll say things which become very small steps. There is no grandiose kind of planning. There is a testing of the waters.

We view ourselves as venture capitalists. We are people investing money into the life of a street person. *the back door* contracts for a total of 24 months with each person. At first, the risk seemed great and the first three months are the riskiest. We have found that for the first three months, participants are testing the sincerity of *the back door* to see whether or not its program is legitimate. Somewhere between the third and the fourth month this idea of contracting begins to become a serious thing. The participant turns around and says, "There's something going on here. How come I can trust people who I've always been told you're not supposed to trust? These people still give me the $15 even if I lie to them."

The fourth, fifth, and sixth months, begin to become less and less of a risk. It's then that the participant often turns around and begins to take more and more ownership for this contracting process and ultimately the planning process.

If there are problems with drugs and alcohol, it's usually within the fourth to sixth months that it is identified by the participant. If there are going to be some treatment issues, those things need to be dealt with between six and ten months. Settlement issues are recurring. The participants say they are out to find their own place. Getting actual longer-term housing is common around the tenth, eleventh and twelfth months. About the thirteenth or the fourteenth month is the time when the person really begins to settle down. Settling down is the result of a process which means taking a job seriously and looking at school as something helpful, not just as a meal ticket because of some schooling grant.

We find that by the time the participant gets to their 24th month, they're not really settled, but they're ready to settle. They're not really in a position to put their life together, but they're in a position where they have their own bed, their own place to go, and if they need to cry, they cry into their own pillow. If their life crashes, they have their own space to go back to. They crash there. Problem solving and facing stability questions become a part of their nature and are a much safer process than in their first months. In the first, second, and third months, when they crashed, they usually crashed back into a drug, alcohol, or prostitution environment, in which the street is still very vicious, and predominates every aspect of their planning.

The 24 months doesn't really say that someone has graduated from contracting. After twenty-four months the person reaches a point where he or she can go into the entry-level stages of life and feel comfortable being there. They can go into some of the programming or can go into some of the elements of community and say, "Yes, I know it's okay for me to be here, even if I'm only a visitor. It's still okay for me to be here."

Today after twelve years we are stronger than we've ever been in the understanding that people come to contract, taking responsibility for their own lives, rather than coming to *the back door* to meet a person who can tell them what to do with their lives. If there's a success story to be told concerning *the back door,* the crucial statement would be: people come here to say, "Yes, I want to take control of my own life," fully knowing that the variables all around them could be things which are too difficult to deal with. Nonetheless, there is still hope. There is still an understanding that maybe, just maybe, things can be different. So, the contract, in the midst of all the experimentation, has stayed the same.

At a service club meeting one day a man stood and criticized the bonus and contracting process. I asked him what business he was in. He said oil. I then asked him how many gushers he got when exploring for oil. Would you get one in ten? He said he could only dream of that kind of success. Many times I hear people say, if you can help only one person, it is worth it. I told the oil man my business is not much different than his. I am not promised a gusher, but if one doesn't drill, one will never find out if there is oil in the ground. I say the same thing. At times we go through some very hard ground, other times we go through soft ground, sometimes all we hit is gas. (This conversation happened when gas was less valuable.) The reality is that we land a gusher seven out of ten times. We call ourselves venture capitalists investing in people for a better society. Now the risk isn't questioned because the return has become so great.

Funding and fund raising
as part of the experiment

When we started *the back door* in 1988 all startup funds were donated to the project. In 1989 our goal, as previously stated, was to raise one third of the funds from the government sector, one third from individual donations, and one third of the funds from the business and corporate sector.

A donation and grant basis was viewed as the appropriate way to finance this project. This decision was arrived at because many said that's the way it's done. Wherever we went, processes had been created to ask for money. The impression was that there is a way to do this, now do it. One of the things we discovered was just how large the gap was between what the system says it wants to do and what actually gets accomplished.

In respect to the discussion with Social Services, we applied for a "Block Grant". It was then acknowledged that a Block Grant could not be given due to the fact that we were working with people with a transient housing status or who lived at a hostel. These people typically did not qualify for Social Assistance benefits, hence they were not in the system. Subsequently, a fee for service concept was arrived at. As potential participants approached Social Services they would qualify for assistance and *the back door* would qualify to receive a fee to contract with the participant. Once again it is to be admitted that problems existed with this concept:

63

1. Without a permanent address potential participants would not be accepted for Social Assistance, and *the back door* did not qualify for a fee for service.

2. Some participants had already been under suspension of benefits from Social Services. Individual social workers refused to approve them for *the back door* participation even though this had been the agreed upon target population.

During its first year, *the back door* went to Social Services attempting to apply for funding to be used for its second year. We believed because we had been a part of the initial ongoing discussions that this was an acceptable process. We believed we were in dialogue with government to discover a process which could work with what had become a very difficult population. We were not to be judged as if we were a completed project. We were entering together into an experiment. It turned out *the back door* was doing an experiment. The government was not.

A great deal of time and energy was spent in negotiating with the government for funding. In the end, Alberta Career Development and Employment came through. The ongoing philosophical differences between Social Services and Career Development created unbelievable blocks for us as we tried to seek funding. Initially, an employee of Career Development sat on our Board of Directors. It was never anticipated that if a wholistic approach was taken when working with this population, the territorialism of departments could and would be so destructive. Despite the conflicts, by the beginning of 1989 we were able to go back to the initial foundation to say, "Yes, we have these kinds of pledges." Because of these funds, the initial donation was then cut back.

In 1990, however, major changes occurred to government policies on funding both medical and educational programs. Initially these changes seemed insignificant to the average person but they were devastating to those who were working in "safety net social programs." Being toward the bottom of the pecking order for funding, merely dropped us off the bottom of whatever lists were out there. Schools, hospitals, universities and colleges just shifted their fund raising machinery to what they perceived as smaller markets. Since we were new and on the fringe, we and others like us were pushed out first. Because of this shift, certain social clubs, service clubs and businesses would come back to us and say, "We're sorry we can't give you the donation this year. The Children's Hospital can give us more visibility. If we have more visibility, we'll be able to sell more tickets. If we sell more tickets, we can raise more funds. With more tickets sold, we can help more people and after all that's what this is all about."

We struggled with more than fund raising. We also struggled because it wasn't just an issue of the government changing directions. *the back door* started as a community project with community people. It arose out of people in the community saying there has to be a way to do something that isn't happening in the system. In at least one way *the back door* represents the dilemma of grass roots people saying there is a way to help. *the back door* process was developed in a grass roots environment, not one in which political whims and partnerships dominate. This project was developed in the open where the press, the community and the government were well aware of what was happening. It was not a project mandated by government. It was mandated by a growing concern in the community that problems were getting out of hand.

Another dimension to consider was the role of the church. Many churches were skeptical of coming behind a community project as opposed to a church project. We were very up front with the fact that this was not a religious program, this was not a Bible study, this was not a church program. *the back door* was a community based program. My role, despite being a clergyman, was very simply to start the project, develop it, and bring it to the point of its own stability. At the same time we were wrestling with asking the churches for support. There were many people within the community who identified *the back door* as a church program because I am an ordained clergyman. At the same time we were told by non-church funding bodies "we don't fund church projects."

There was just as much of a gap between funders, communities, churches as there was between government departments. People were very willing to have meetings but very reluctant to actually cover costs. No matter how hard we tried to explain the gaps that we were falling through we were struggling. As early as 1991 and 1992 we were facing severe economic realities.

At one point I brought the staff in and told them if they wanted their jobs, they had to become a part of the fundraising team. Some responded that they were professionals and would be able to find jobs in other agencies where grants were available to pay them appropriately for their professional status. These staff had been extremely committed and supportive people throughout the years they were with us. But there also came with this sense of professionalism, expectations which created an ongoing economic pressure.

We had created a project where street youth took us at our word. They believed in us and trusted us. For us the question was very simple. Were we willing to work for our own survival as hard as they were working to get off the street?

One of the crucial questions at that time was "Do we take a look at who we are in relation to what Revenue Canada calls 'A Rescue Mission'?" Rescue Missions have a tendency to have staff go out and raise their own funds so that each staff member can then survive. The process is called "deputation." This works for missionaries and church projects but would it work in the community? As we tried this approach we found donations were being made to cover individual staff but then money was not coming in to run the project.

We began to raise the question: "How do we as staff, those of us who are left, fund this project?" We were in a situation where we didn't know what to do. At that time, a person gave us nine small vending machines. This person told us, "Just go out, place, and stock these vending machines and take the money from them." We started with those nine vending machines. We found that if we took the money from them, pro-rated a portion to project costs, another portion to product costs, another portion to maintenance, and a final portion to purchase more vending machines, that it could work. What followed is perhaps another whole story. Vending became a project within a project. It became a model for us to follow as we developed yet more ventures toward our goal of self sufficiency.

We also used the concept of sponsorships. A $1500 sponsorship would cover the cost of one young person taking one hundred steps off the street. The sponsorship of $120 equals the cost of helping one young person take steps off the street for one month, a $15 sponsorship covers the cost of each person taking one step. While donations still remain a very important part of the funding process, special events and promotions account for the lion's share of non-participant costs.

What others have said:

TAKEN FROM EVALUATION &
PROGRAM RECOMMENDATION
by Pacific Rim Research Team
Gerry Clark and Kristin Shannon

June 17, 1991

The United Way: Gerry Clark, President
Halifax, Nova Scotia

Pacific Rim Research: Kristin Shannon, Chairman
Sausalito, California U.S.A.
Vancouver, British Columbia,

Some summary thoughts:

Taken together, the levels of trust and responsibility support some very significant growth in the self-esteem of the participants. The results of The Back Door go beyond changes in external behavior; the program affects deeply held attitudes and values which in turn alter the lives of the youth who participate.

The Back Door system of goals ("STEPS") and incentives ("BONUSES") makes frequent use of written CONTRACTS with individual participants. The CONTRACTS spell out the mutual commitments and bonuses, are kept in open files, and are modified as progress is made. The result of the CONTRACT system is twofold: as each external "STEP" is achieved and bonused, the participant not only achieves a measurable result, but experiences a sense of increasing integrity and self-worth as they learn to make and keep agreements with themselves and others.

While warm human relations are clearly part of the formula, the incentives for progress are not tied to politics, favoritism, or a staff need to feel parental. The written straightforward CONTRACT keeps the expectations on the table for both the staff and the participants. From the perspective of the interview team the contracts, are in fact, "a clean deal."

The unique adaptation of the CONTRACT method to help solve the social and economic problems associated with street life seems very effective, and worth replicating. Rather than creating yet another institutional half-way house or a separate world with different symbols and priorities from the mainstream of society, The Back Door program is blunt about recognizing "success" in the same way that employed people receive recognition: BONUSES are for money, not gold stars.

For four hundred years the western system of charity and welfare has emphasized either "handouts" (which undercut self-esteem and initiative) or sheltered workshops (which utilize different incentives than the mainstream economy). The traditional message to the recipients is that they are "not OK" and may never "make it" into an economically (and socially) acceptable position.

The review team finds that The Back Door's use of CONTRACT has been an important lever in creating a new model. The underlying message of the CONTRACT process is that "learning how to earn money, and keep agreements (with yourself and others) will help you achieve a valuable sense of independence in our society."

Findings: The review team is pleased to report that, in our opinion, The Back Door has initiated an innovative and effective program which we find to be successful in helping street youth. Not only is the specific program of value, but the CONTRACT system itself should be evaluated for export to other kinds of programs.

The Back Door is a success. It is also rightly a focus of pride for the people involved in the agency, particularly the participants.

EXTERNAL REVIEW April - May, 1996
Dr. Dan Offord
Canadian Institute for Advanced Research
Toronto, Ontario

The Back Door is to be contrasted with most mainstream social service agencies addressing the needs of street youth. What is obvious is that The Back Door differs from mainstream agencies in many important respects. It is not a mainstream agency but it is out to one side - a fringe agency for want of a better term. It could be likened to venture capital in the business world.

After talking with four participants who were either currently enrolled in the program or who have completed it but still keep in touch with The Back Door. Dr. Dan Offord says all four were extremely complimentary about the program. They made statements such as "the best thing that ever happened to me". As one might expect, they commented positively on the special aspects of the program as noted in the preceding table, and then talked about the characteristics that turned them off of the usual programs to help street youth.

It is clear that for these four youth, The Back Door has played a unique role in changing their developmental pathways in late adolescence from destructive trajectories (including possibly death) to ones that do not include the street and generate feelings of hopefulness and productivity in these youth.

Selected Characteristics of The Back Door and Mainstream Social Service Agencies	
The Back Door	**Mainstream Agencies**
* committed to helping youth get off the street	*usually committed to enriching the life quality of youth while they are on the street.
*located away from the streets	*located adjacent to the streets
*emphasizes empowerment and taking charge of one's life	*centres on helping by providing services, e.g.., housing, counseling
*focuses on steps, contracts and bonuses	*may focus on steps, usually not on contracts and never give money to participants
*quick response time	*may involve paper work and waiting lists
*comfortable with an on-and-off relationship over a period of time	*may be more stringent about admission and discharge criteria and length of involvement.
*small, familiar and deeply committed staff	*large, changing staff with varying levels of commitment.

The Back Door does accept a limited number of students for their clinical placements. This training element of The Back Door could be expanded to include, not just more students, but also staff from mainstream agencies.

The Back Door is a unique, effective program for a portion of street youth who want to get off the street and move towards a more traditional lifestyle. It deserves ongoing, enthusiastic support.

In Conclusion

The title of this book, _the back door, an experiment or an alternative_ arose out of the process of writing it. In 1988 we perceived ourselves to be an experiment. Today we are no longer an experiment. The contract/bonus process has offered a potential alternative to traditional ways of thinking and working with this population. The contract emphasizes personal ownership for change while nurturing the capacity and values each person has for change.

In 1988 the use of money as an incentive, the use of a contract for accountability, and the choice to believe in people were seen as quite contentious ideas within social welfare circles. The idea of applying everyday principles taken from the work force and home life really did work. At the core of the issue is the belief that a human person can and will change.

This is not a grandiose plan to recreate society in someone's image. It is a statement that people live in society. Sometimes society gets out of control. Sometimes society gets too much in control. All we ask is there be a balance allowing for people to discover their personal sense of direction within a framework of others doing the same. With a little more personal responsibility, trust and dignity we might be able to see a safer place for our children at least for one more generation. _the back door_ is offered to you as an alternative, a means to encourage more responsibility and self-respect.